Toby and Trish
and the Amazing Book of
MATTHEW

Text copyright © Peggy Hewitt 2000
Illustrations copyright © Tom Hewitt 2000
The author asserts the moral right to be identified as the
author of this work.
Published by **The Bible Reading Fellowship**
Peter's Way, Sandy Lane West
Oxford OX4 6HG
ISBN 1 84101 127 4
First edition 2000
10 9 8 7 6 5 4 3 2 1 0
Acknowledgments
Scripture quotations are taken from the Good News Bible
published by The Bible Societies/HarperCollins Publishers
Ltd UK © American Bible Society, 1966, 1971, 1976, 1992.
A catalogue record for this book is available from the
British Library.
Printed and bound in Great Britain
by Omnia Books Ltd, Glasgow

Toby and Trish
(and Boomerang!)
and the Amazing Book of
MATTHEW

Peggy Hewitt
Illustrated by Tom Hewitt

Welcome to the Amazing Book of MATTHEW!

A sk a grown-up to let you have a look at a £5 note—or you may even have one of your own. Above the picture of the Queen are the words 'Bank of England', and below these—look carefully—it says, 'I promise to pay the bearer, on demand, the sum of Five Pounds'. It's signed by somebody important at the Bank of England.

A £5 note is only worthless paper, but that promise makes it valuable. It means we can use it to buy what we need. A promise is important.

By reading Matthew's Gospel, we can learn about the promises made by God to his people over hundreds of years. It explains how God did exactly as he promised when he sent Jesus to be our special friend. When God says he will do something, he does it.

Who's who!
Matthew 1:1-17

*So then, there were fourteen
generations from Abraham
to David, and fourteen from
David to the exile in Babylon,
and fourteen from then to the
birth of the Messiah. (Verse 17)*

In an adventure story, often everything works out when the right
person turns up at the right time and
does the right thing. Maybe they flick a
switch to stop the world being blown up,
or parachute from a plane or capture the 'baddie'.

Matthew's Gospel is an amazing adventure story.
God had promised King David, hundreds of years
before, that God's chosen one would come from
David's family. All those people with the strange
names were the chosen one's distant relatives. He
would be David's great-great- (and lots more
'greats') grandson. And now here he was.

Jesus was the right person, who came exactly
when God had planned it, to show us just how much
God loves us.

Now read on for the whole exciting story.

A special baby
Matthew
1:18-20

My mum said I was special—but this baby is extra, extra special!

This was how the birth of Jesus Christ took place. His mother Mary was engaged to Joseph, but before they were married, she found out that she was going to have a baby by the Holy Spirit. (Verse 18)

Sometimes when we get some special news, it's hard for us to take it in at first. But when we do, it makes a tremendous difference to us. Read Luke chapter 1 verses 26–33 and find out how God told Mary about her special baby. News like this had never been heard before. It sounded impossible. Yet Mary accepted what the angel told her—no matter what other people thought.

But Joseph didn't understand at first. He was too worried by the way things looked. Although he loved Mary, he felt he had to do what everybody expected him to do. Until God spoke to him too! Then he learned that sometimes God does things in a different way.

Mary and Joseph's lives were completely changed when God chose them to care for this special baby.

6

A special name
Matthew 1:20-24

'She will have a son, and you will name him Jesus—because he will save his people from their sins.' (Verse 21)

I'm named after my great-uncle Tobias

Names are very important. We know people at first by their names. (Come to think of it, we know *things* by their names, too.) Some names have a particular meaning. My name, Peggy, means 'little pearl'. Peter means 'rock'. Try to find out if your name has another meaning.

We've read today that Mary's special baby will have two names—two names so special that the whole of the rest of the Bible is written about them.

'*Jesus*'—the one who will show us how much God loves us.

'*Immanuel*'—he will do this because he is actually God himself. He's the one everybody has been waiting for for so long: God with us.

We need to think about these special names as we read Matthew's Gospel.

Message in the stars
Matthew 2:1-8

They asked,
'Where is the
baby born to be
the king of the
Jews? We saw his star
when it came up in the east, and we
have come to worship him.' (Verse 2)

Not long ago, on television, there were some programmes about the planets and the stars— what they are and what they are made of. And the man said a lovely thing: 'We are all really made out of stardust.' Just imagine: you, me, everybody—we are all part of what God made at the very beginning.

Because of this, the men who studied the stars knew what this star—'his star'—was all about. Something tremendous had happened and they came looking for it.

And because of this, we too can become part of this first wonderful Christmas. We can make a journey in our hearts to the place chosen by God for Jesus to be born. Not to a king's palace in Jerusalem, but to the little town of Bethlehem.

The first Christmas present
Matthew 2:9–12

And so they left, and on their way they saw the same star they had seen in the east. When they saw it, how happy they were, what joy was theirs! It went ahead of them until it stopped over the place where the child was. (Verses 9–10)

What a journey these wise men had. Travelling mostly by night, sometimes over strange and difficult country, they must have *known* that the star they followed would lead them to what they were searching for.

It was not at the king's palace in Jerusalem! Then, when the star set off again, they must have *known* that something really special was waiting for them. They felt so happy that maybe they sang as they travelled.

The star stopped at Bethlehem, where King David himself had been born. And these wise men knelt in front of baby Jesus and gave him presents of gold, frankincense and myrrh. Their search was over.

They *knew* they had found God, and they *knew* why he had come.

Matthew 1:1—2:12

Things to do

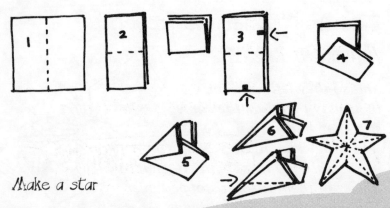

Make a star

To make a star, fold a square of paper in half (from left to right), and then in half again. Open out the second fold and mark halfway along the bottom edge and halfway down the side of the top square.

Fold the paper so that the two marks touch. Fold the top corner down to form a point on the left-hand side. Fold the bottom corner up, keeping the point on the left. Cut as shown by the dotted line in the diagram. Now open out your star!

Escape route
Matthew 2:13-15

Joseph got up, took the child and his mother, and left during the night for Egypt. (Verse 14)

Moving house can be quite exciting. Cups, glasses, dishes, all to be wrapped in tissue paper and put into boxes, pictures taken off walls, toys and books stuffed into bags, clothes packed away. It takes days, and you usually find you need something that's packed at the bottom of one of those boxes. But which? Then the removal van arrives and you watch everything disappearing inside it. Great fun.

It wasn't like that for Joseph and Mary and Jesus. They hadn't got most of the things that we collect around us. It was all done quickly, quietly, in the middle of the night, leaving their friends without saying 'Goodbye'. Just a word from God to Joseph and they were away, out of Herod's reach. Because they obeyed God, their lives were saved.

11

Back home to Nazareth

Matthew 2:16-23

Joseph made his home in a town named Nazareth. And so what the prophets had said came true: 'He will be called a Nazarene.' (Verse 23)

Near where I live, there's a castle that's over eight hundred years old. Exciting things have happened there—battles and sieges, banquets and jousting— and famous people have lived there. Deep down are the dungeons where awful things happened.

You can look round this castle. School parties especially like the ancient toilet—just a hole in the wall! And to help you understand what it's all about, there's a guidebook.

Matthew uses the Old Testament as a guidebook to help us to understand God's plan, over hundreds of years, for the coming of Jesus. The prophets, who were close to God, have prepared us for what will happen... some things lovely and exciting, other things awful. But it is all known to God, even before it happens, just as what we do is known to God even before we do it.

John prepares the way
Matthew 3:1-12

He has his winnowing shovel with him to thresh out all the grain. He will gather his wheat into his barn, but he will burn the chaff in a fire that never goes out. (Verse 12)

A long time ago, some farms had only two rooms. The family lived in one room and the grain was beaten, or threshed, in the other—the barn. The barn doors were flung open, the useless bits blew away and the good grain was left. This was called the 'threshing floor' and the doorway between the rooms was the 'threshold'.

If I promise to behave—can I come in?

We still use that word today. Now 'threshold' means that we're about to go from one room to another, or from an old way of thinking, and being, to a new one.

We've all done things we wish we hadn't. If only we could start again! John came to *say* that we could be forgiven; Jesus came actually *to forgive us*. If we are ready to step across the 'threshold', we can start a new way of thinking, and being, with Jesus as our friend.

Jesus is baptized
Matthew 3:13-17

I am going in in a minute— when I've thought about it!

At that time Jesus arrived from Galilee and came to John at the Jordan to be baptized by him. (Verse 13)

Close your eyes and pretend you're actually there by the River Jordan. It's a hot and sunny day and there's a great crowd of people. Everybody is watching one man, John the Baptist.

Then another man arrives and suddenly everybody is watching him. Not many people know who he is, yet—but John knows. It is Jesus, ready to start his work of love. Try to imagine how John is feeling as Jesus waits in line to be baptized—by him.

There's a quietness as Jesus steps into the water—then a deeper hush. No one moves. God is here in a very special way. He is preparing Jesus for his work ahead.

Now... just sit quietly for a moment. God is here with us now.

I'm having a hard time—
they've gone out
and left me!

A hard time
Matthew 4:1-11

Then the Devil left Jesus; and angels came and helped him. (Verse 11)

Have you ever noticed that when you've had a really great time, it's often followed by a difficult time when you struggle a bit?

Jesus had just seen and heard and felt God when he was baptized. Now here he was, in an empty, bleak place, all alone, to think and pray about his work and what lay at the end of it. Surely God would be with him there? But it seemed not. It was the devil who kept him company.

But God only allowed Jesus to be tempted to show us that Jesus is far and above anything the devil can do. And when it was over, God sent him comfort.

When we're having our bad times, God hasn't forgotten us. And in the end he will help us—if we'll let him.

Matthew 2:13—4:11
Things to do

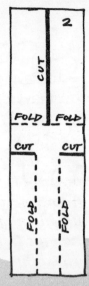

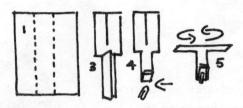

A chopper that really flies!

You can't make a dove that flies, but you *can* make a helicopter.

Cut an A4 piece of paper into three strips. Take one of the strips and cut as shown in the diagram. Fold in the sides of the bottom half, then fold up the bottom 2.5 cm and secure with a paper-clip.

On the top half, fold one 'blade' back and the other 'blade' forward. Test your helicopter, then write on the blades God's message which came down from heaven.

Even nearer
Matthew 4:12-17

I can hear the car! Toby and Trish are about to arrive!

From that time Jesus began to preach his message: 'Turn away from your sins, because the Kingdom of heaven is near!'
(Verse 17)

Now where have we heard that message before? Only two or three days ago. And who said it? Look again at chapter 3 verse 2 for the answers. 'The kingdom of heaven is near.' And who arrived on the scene almost immediately after John had said it? *Jesus.*

Now John is in prison (we'll come to that story later) and Jesus himself is giving the same message in Capernaum: 'The kingdom of heaven is near'—even nearer.

Two different places: Jordan and Capernaum. The same message: 'The kingdom of heaven is near.' The same person is there in both places—Jesus.

The kingdom of heaven is wherever Jesus is... Jordan... Capernaum... or in your heart.

Four fishermen friends
Matthew 4:18-25

At once they left their nets and went with him. (Verse 20)

My favourite place for holidays is Greece. I love to wander round the little harbours and watch the fishermen mending their nets. A net is very important to a fisherman—it's huge, wider than a tennis court, and it's essential that there are no tears in it. You can guess why.

The fisherman spends hours going over the net and repairing it. He sits with bare feet, holding part of the net between his toes to spread it out and inspect it, then he pulls it through his toes to the next bit. He needs lots of patience and care to do this.

The four fishermen friends were happy to leave their nets behind and follow Jesus. In their new life they would need the same patience and care.

Happiness is...
Matthew 5:1–12

School breaks up tomorrow!

'Happy are those whose greatest desire is to do what God requires; God will satisfy them fully!' (Verse 6)

'Hey-ho, hey-ho, it's off to work we go.' You'll probably know the story of Snow White and the Seven Dwarfs. One of the dwarfs was called Happy because he always had a twinkly, rosy face and a big smile. But that wasn't real happiness because, until the end of the story, he'd never known anything that was difficult, that could make him sad. His happiness was only 'skin deep'.

Real happiness comes from deep inside you. It comes from doing what God wants you to do, at home, at school, wherever you are. It even means feeling sad for others or when things go wrong—but knowing that God is there. It means being brave when you don't feel it, because God will help you. Happiness is knowing who you are, and who God is. And then you'll really be able to smile.

Taste, sight and feeling
Matthew 5:13–16 and 21–25

'You are like salt for the whole human race. But if salt loses its saltiness, there is no way to make it salty again. It has become worthless, so it is thrown out and people trample on it.' (Verse 13)

Jesus lived in a very hot country, and in very hot countries it's important to eat a little salt to keep healthy. A long time ago, in hot countries, people sometimes used salt instead of money to pay for things—it was so precious.

Some people put a little bit of salt in food to bring out the flavour (if you can taste the salt, you've used too much, and that's not good). Food without salt can sometimes be dull and dreary and boring.

A life without Jesus can also be dull and dreary and boring. Jesus came to show us how to live a caring and an exciting life. And other people should notice the difference that Jesus makes to us and want to share it.

Don't 'get even'
Matthew 5:38-42

'But now I tell you: do not take revenge on someone who wrongs you.' (Verse 39a)

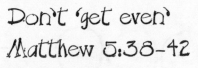

Maybe you've watched 'Tom and Jerry' on television. Jerry is a bright little mouse who takes great delight in making Tom's life difficult. Tom is a not-so-bright cat who spends all his time and energy trying to get even, or trying to get the better of Jerry. He never manages it. Instead, after lots of adventures that make *us* laugh, he's left not knowing who he is or where he is. Jerry sits preening his whiskers and Tom is exhausted and flattened.

Sometimes, somebody really gets our goat—they might even do things to hurt us. But getting even hurts us still more. We forget who we are, waste a lot of time and energy—and often we're left feeling exhausted and flattened.

Things to do

Happiness is...

At the beginning of chapter 5 of Matthew's amazing book, there are nine verses that start with 'Happy are...' Cut out nine circles, each about 5 cm across. On one side draw a smiley face and on the other side write 'Happiness is...' and put what Jesus said in your own words. String the circles together and hang them up in your bedroom.

Toby + Trish — Not happy rabbits

Happiness is chasing rabbits and not getting my nose stuck in a rabbit hole

Love your enemies
Matthew 5:43-47

*'And if you speak only
to your friends, have
you done anything
out of the ordinary?
Even the pagans do that!'
(Verse 47)*

Loving is hard when it's a one-way ticket

It's fairly easy to love someone who loves you. You feel safe and you know you won't get hurt. Loving them comes naturally and you know that the love you give will be given back to you in return. Anybody can love his or her friends.

But how about loving somebody who *doesn't* love you—somebody you don't even like? That's more difficult. When you love, you open up your heart, and that means you can get hurt inside. It's a risk. Giving out love is not easy when there's no love coming the other way. And besides, why should we?

We should love those who don't love us because Jesus asks us to; but mainly because he himself loved them. As his enemies nailed him on to the cross, he forgave them. *And he loved them.*

Our Father
Matthew 6:1-4
and 7-13

'This, then, is how you should pray: "Our Father in heaven: May your holy name be honoured".' (Verse 9)

Words, words, words. They spill out of us like water out of a fountain. Maybe if they were rationed and we could only use a certain number each day, we would think carefully before we spoke. Then our words would really mean something—they would be important.

'Our Father.' Just two words that mean so much. Not '*my*' Father. God is the Father of *everyone* who tries to do and to be what he wants. Therefore all these people are our brothers and sisters. 'Father.' Someone who knows us and loves us, someone we can trust and who wants us to love him.

Count the words in the prayer that Matthew sets out for us, from verse 9b to 13. There aren't many but they mean everything. 'Our Father'! That is amazing.

Riches that last
Matthew 6:19-23

I'd take my snorkel and flippers

'Store up riches for yourselves in heaven, where moths and rust cannot destroy, and robbers cannot break in and steal. For your heart will always be where your riches are.' (Verses 20–21)

There's a radio programme called 'Desert Island Discs' which is all a big pretend. A famous person is asked which eight pieces of music they would take, and why, if they were 'cast away' on a desert island all by themselves. The music is played—and then comes the difficult bit. They're also allowed to take one thing that they love the most.

What would you choose? We've all got so much— drawers, cupboards, shelves full. And if we're not careful, these 'treasures' of ours become so important that they take up all our time and love. But they won't last for ever. Bicycles rust, books fall apart, clothes wear out. Then what?

If we love Jesus first, more than anything else, he is our treasure that will last for ever.

Let go!
Matthew 6:24-30

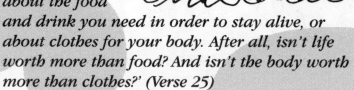

'This is why I tell you not to be worried about the food and drink you need in order to stay alive, or about clothes for your body. After all, isn't life worth more than food? And isn't the body worth more than clothes?' (Verse 25)

I can remember learning to swim. It was years ago and I was so tense and strung up, just like knots in rope, that what should have been fun wasn't. I was wearing armbands but I was so worried I might disappear under the water that I kept one foot on the bottom. There—I've said it.

Slowly I realized, as I hopped along, that the water was trying to hold me up if I'd just relax and trust it. So I lifted *both* feet, stopped thrashing about and... I was swimming. So I took off the armbands and realized how wonderful swimming is.

Jesus wants us to relax and enjoy today without worrying about what *might* happen tomorrow. Trust him. Then you'll know how wonderful life really is.

Something in your eye?
Matthew 7:1-5

That's the last time I look up when a pigeon flies overhead!

'Why, then, do you look at the speck in your brother's eye, and pay no attention to the log in your own eye?' (Verse 3)

It's awful when you get something in your eye—maybe an eyelash or a speck of dust. It feels huge, your eyes water and you can't see properly.

Jesus liked a joke and he's talking here about somebody walking about with a log in their eye. Just imagine! Yet you and I do it a lot, in a way. Finding fault with others and ignoring our own faults (which may be worse) makes us feel good.

Jesus says, 'Take the "log" out of your own eye first. Then walk all around yourself and look at *yourself* with clear eyes.' Wow! Maybe we're not so perfect after all. Maybe we should sort out our own faults before we jump in on other people's.

Once we realize how much we need God's forgiveness, we'll find it easier not to find fault with others.

Matthew 5:43—7:5

Things to do

Why worry?

Draw a black cloud with 'worry' written on it on one side of a folded card. Underneath the cloud, draw

a cartoon picture of yourself looking miserable. On the other side, draw the sun and colour it with a bright yellow crayon.

Next, find the reason why we should never worry by looking in chapter 6 verses 25–34 of Matthew's amazing book. Choose the bit you like best and write it in.

Toby + Trish — Worrying spell

Ask, seek, knock
Matthew 7:7–12

'For everyone who asks will receive, and anyone who seeks will find, and the door will be opened to those who knock.' (Verse 8)

Isaac Watts was always asking, 'Why?' because things interested him. One day he saw a kettle boiling and noticed the lid bouncing up and down. 'Why? What makes it do that?' Eventually he discovered steam power (which is dangerous if not handled properly). It made wheels go round in machines to produce all sorts of things. Then George Stephenson came along and made steam power push wheels on rails. Yes! Steam trains.

Jesus has all sorts of wonderful things just waiting for us. But we must want to know, ask questions, and pray. Every day can be like opening a new door to new experiences with Jesus. If we look for him—there he is. And he will give us power to live a life that is adventurous and exciting.

22

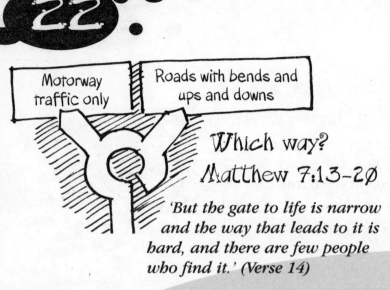

Motorway traffic only

Roads with bends and ups and downs

Which way?
Matthew 7:13-20

'But the gate to life is narrow and the way that leads to it is hard, and there are few people who find it.' (Verse 14)

There are two roads going out of England and way up into Scotland. One is a brand new three-lane motorway. It's like any other motorway—straight, fast and easy. But if you're driving, you feel like a hamster on its treadmill. Where am I? If you're not driving, you nod off through boredom.

The other, narrower, 'scenic' route is different—more fun. You go up and down and round corners. You feel you're actually travelling somewhere. It takes you through little villages and sometimes you actually have to think which way to go. You might even get lost, but there are plenty of signposts if you do. It's an adventure.

Following Jesus is like this. It's fun. If you get lost, he will bring you back to the right way. It's harder—you actually have to think. But it's an adventure.

Good foundations
Matthew 7:24-28

'The rain poured down, the rivers overflowed, and the wind blew hard against that house. But it did not fall, because it was built on rock.' (Verse 25)

There was once a man who worked for a builder. Just before the man retired, the builder sent for him. 'One more job—I want you to build a house,' he said. Now the man was resentful. He didn't think he'd been rewarded enough for his years of hard work.

So he built the house badly. The doors didn't fit, the roof leaked, the floors creaked, and even before it was finished the walls were cracking because of poor foundations. At last it was finished. 'The house is yours,' said the builder. 'It's your reward for all your hard work. Go and live in it.'

How are we building our lives? We are the ones who have to live them. Will we 'crack' when hard times come—or are our lives built on the firm rock of the love of Jesus?

A stranger's faith
Matthew 8:5-13

When Jesus heard this, he was surprised and said to the people following him, 'I tell you, I have never found anyone in Israel with faith like this.'
(Verse 10)

A heavy lorry, piled high with goods, was rumbling through New York on its eight huge wheels. It came to a bridge, almost made it underneath—then got stuck. The driver and his mate got out, looked, and couldn't think what to do. A traffic jam piled up behind; a crowd gathered.

Then a little girl ran to the driver and said, 'Let the air out of the tyres.' They did, and the lorry, lower now, drove slowly under the bridge. Sometimes the most unexpected people can see what's happening and understand it.

The Roman officer was an 'outsider', a stranger, yet the minute he saw Jesus he understood what Jesus could do. He believed.

Maybe we need to take a new look at Jesus ourselves, to understand just what he can do.

Lord of the winds and waves
Matthew 8:23-27

'Why are you so frightened?' Jesus answered. 'How little faith you have!' Then he got up and ordered the winds and the waves to stop, and there was a great calm. (Verse 26)

I can remember the first time I flew in an aeroplane. I was so excited, and a little bit frightened. When we took off, I was amazed that this great heavy thing could fly like a bird. Since then I've flown many times and it doesn't seem quite so exciting and amazing, which is a shame.

When Jesus did these wonderful things that Matthew tells us about, they were new and exciting. People were amazed. Maybe now that we know these stories so well, we're not amazed any more, which is a shame.

But *be* there—on that boat, in that storm, with those waves towering over you. *Be* frightened. Then hear the voice of Jesus, and feel that special quietness. *Then* you'll be amazed.

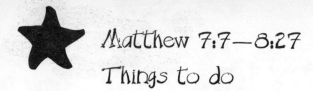

Matthew 7:7—8:27

Things to do

Even if...

Colour in this drawing of you and your brother, sister or best friend standing in a huge pair of hands. Write the words, 'Peace, be still' on the hands to remind you that Jesus is with you in the storms of life.

CRASH

Toby + Trish — Making waves

Why does Mum wave when she comes to meet me?

Because she's glad to sea you!

First things first
Matthew 9:1-8

Some people brought to him a paralysed man, lying on a bed. When Jesus saw how much faith they had, he said to the paralysed man, 'Courage, my son! Your sins are forgiven.'(Verse 2)

People sometimes talk about 'putting the cart before the horse'. Have you ever seen a cart pulling a horse? Just imagine! It really means that sometimes we put things that are very important into second place and deal with less important things first.

Jesus knew that the most important thing was to make the man better on the *inside*—in his heart, the bit that *didn't* show. So he forgave him everything he had done wrong. Only God, through Jesus, can do that. Then Jesus cured his poor sick body too, the bit that *did* show.

Jesus knows what we need, both in our hearts and in our bodies, and he will deal with it all in the right order—if we are willing to let him.

27

Jesus people
Matthew 9:9-13

> Read the three gospels: Mark, Luke and John

Jesus left that place, and as he walked along, he saw a tax collector, named Matthew, sitting in his office. He said to him, 'Follow me.' Matthew got up and followed him. (Verse 9)

Let's start with a puzzle. Mark, Luke and John. What is missing? *Matthew*, of course. If Matthew had said 'No' to Jesus, there'd have been a great hole in the Bible and we wouldn't be reading this book now. Good thing he didn't!

All day Matthew sat there, collecting tax money to give to the Romans. Sometimes he even took too much and kept some for himself—which made him very unpopular. He was rich but he wasn't happy. His friends had the same sort of jobs, and they weren't happy either.

Then Jesus came along, and Matthew's life was changed. First he wanted to share Jesus with his friends, the sad and unpopular people who really needed him. And Jesus loved them all.

All things new
Matthew 9:14-17

'No one patches up an old coat with a piece of new cloth, for the new patch will shrink and make an even bigger hole in the coat.' (Verse 16)

It's hopeless. We'll have to put in for a new dog

I wonder how many times the word 'new' appears in the *New* Testament. A lot, I think.

New things are exciting, full of surprises, and we need to look at them in a new way. A new day is different from yesterday, different from tomorrow... let's not waste it. New babies, new bicycles, new clothes. A new book to write in at school—let's be neat, no crossings out (at first).

The *Old* Testament is full of rules about what we should do and how we should do it. But now Jesus himself has come and the *New* Testament is about his love for you and me. A new way of life, excitement, surprises. Jesus is offering us much more than just a set of old rules—he's offering us a *new beginning*.

Hand in hand with Jesus
Matthew 9:18-26

But as soon as the people had been put out, Jesus went into the girl's room and took hold of her hand, and she got up. (Verse 25)

There's a funny poem by Edward Lear which starts, 'The owl and the pussy-cat went to sea in a beautiful pea-green boat. They took some honey and plenty of money wrapped up in a five-pound note'. It finishes, 'And hand in hand on the edge of the sand they danced by the light of the moon'—a happy ending.

If you're feeling sad, or lost, or lonely, or a bit confused and don't know what's happening, you feel much better if someone takes hold of your hand.

The girl we read about had had an unusual experience. The house was full of strangers. What had been going on? But Jesus took hold of her hand and she knew that everything was all right again. It was a happy ending.

The good shepherd
Matthew 9:35-38

As Jesus saw the crowds, his heart was filled with pity for them, because they were worried and helpless, like sheep without a shepherd. (Verse 36)

Sheep look cute, like balls of knitting-wool with a leg at each corner. Unfortunately they sometimes do very silly things. They wander off where they shouldn't, finish up in dangerous places like ledges or gullies and stand there making a big noise until the shepherd finds them. Or they decide the field isn't big enough, or the grass isn't green enough, and push their way out and stand in the middle of the road with cars whizzing past. Other times they just follow each other, no matter where the front one's going.

Sometimes we go our own way, finish up in trouble and make a big noise. Often we blame somebody else.

Jesus knows what is best for us and understands our problems. If we trust him, he will keep us safe.

Things to do

In touch

A woman touched Jesus. Jesus touched the blind man and a little girl...

Show you care by holding someone's hand or putting your arm round their shoulder. If you have a pet, place your hand on it and think caringly about it. Use your teddy if you haven't got a pet—or if your pet is a goldfish!

Toby + Trish | Out of touch

I'd like to get in touch with our great-aunt in Australia

Tricky! You'd have to telephone her yesterday to talk to her today!

Messengers for Jesus
Matthew 10:1-15

'Go and preach, "The Kingdom of heaven is near!"'
(Verse 7)

Have you ever seen a photograph that was so smudgy you couldn't tell what was what? I've taken a few like that. The camera was out of focus—it hadn't been aimed at the right thing in the right way. Result—a mish-mash!

Jesus had given his disciples a diffcult job to do. They'd only be able to do it if they remembered exactly what their aims were and didn't waste time on anything else. They had to keep 'focused'.

'Don't travel too far.' 'Don't get too comfortable and stay where people won't listen to your message.' 'Don't take too much with you—it will slow you down.'

The disciples' instructions were clear—to tell the Jewish people about God's love and to heal them. They had to stay focused on Jesus.

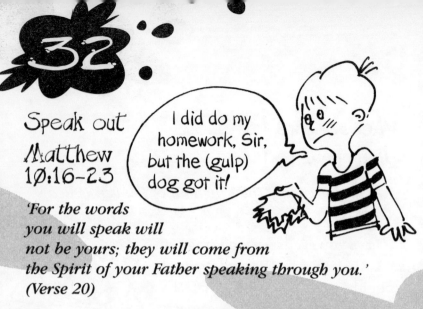

32

Speak out
Matthew 10:16-23

*'For the words
you will speak will
not be yours; they will come from
the Spirit of your Father speaking through you.'*
(Verse 20)

Do you know what it feels like to be 'tongue-tied'? I do. Maybe you've got to apologize to someone, or explain something, or meet somebody you don't know, and words just won't come.

The disciples must have felt like that as they set out to do Jesus' work. How would they cope with what might happen? What words should they use? They were only ordinary people.

There was once a man who had work to do for God and he felt just like that. 'Don't send me—I'm a poor speaker.' His name was Moses. But by letting God speak through him, he became one of the 'greats' of the Old Testament. You can read about him in Exodus chapter 4 verses 10–14.

God knows about our difficulties and he'll show us what do, and say, if we give him the chance.

Precious to God
Matthew 10:26-33

I hope God will love me as much when I've had my hair cut

'As for you, even the hairs of your head have all been counted.' (Verse 30)

Pick up a hairbrush and see if you can count its bristles. You'll need a lot of patience to count them all.

Now, stand in front of the mirror, take hold of a handful of hair, and count the hairs. That really is impossible—there are hundreds just in that one handful. You can't possibly know how many there are all together!

But God knows how many. He loves you so much that he knows every tiny part of you. And that's not all. He loves that boy in your class whom you don't like, and the girl who pushed you off your bike, in just the same way.

Maybe we should try to love them too.

34

Lost... and found
Matthew 10:38-42

If you keep sailing west, you'll fall off the edge!

'Those who try to gain their own life will lose it; but those who lose their life for my sake will gain it.' (Verse 39)

Over five hundred years ago, a boy lived in Italy who had such a dream that not only did he start a new life, he discovered a new world. He was Christopher Columbus.

When he was fourteen, he left his old life behind and began a new, adventurous life as a sailor. But his real dream was to sail far out to the west, where nobody had sailed before. People laughed at him, but he set out, and after dangers and difficulties he not only discovered new and exciting islands, he discovered America—the 'New World'.

When we set out with Jesus, we'll start a new life. It's a voyage of discovery. It won't always be easy, but it will be exciting. We'll discover a whole new world... which is not all that far away.

The coded message
Matthew 11:1-6

I'll see if they get the message...

'How happy are those who have no doubts about me!'
(Verse 6)

Have you ever had a visit from somebody special whom you've been waiting for for a long time? Next day, when you wake up, it's hard to believe it happened.

It was even harder for John. He'd waited a long time for Jesus to come—and then Jesus did come. Now John was in prison. 'Had Jesus really come?' 'Was it really him?' So John sent his disciples to Jesus with lots of questions. 'Look around you,' Jesus answered, 'and stop doubting.' It was a clever answer because it was a coded message.

The long list of wonderful happenings in verse 5 had all been mentioned before—by the prophet Isaiah when he looked towards the coming of God's special one.

John knew this and would therefore know beyond any doubt that Jesus was that special person when he was told what was happening.

Matthew 10:1—11:6

Things to do

Secret agent

In the next village to the one where I live, the Sunday school is called 'Secret Agents'. Read chapter ten of Matthew's amazing book again and decide what mission Jesus is giving *you*. Write down your secret instruction and put the paper in a safe place. Remember, Jesus is with you all the way when you carry out your mission for him!

No pleasing some people
Matthew 11:16–19

I want to eat this chocolate, but I don't want to have none left

'When John came, he fasted and drank no wine, *and everyone said, "He has a demon in him!" When the Son of Man came, he ate and drank, and everyone said, "Look at this man! He is a glutton and a drinker!"' (Verses 18–19)*

Sometimes we can be downright awkward. Maybe Mum wants us to do something in a certain way—so we do it a different way. Often it turns out badly. Or a relative wants to take us somewhere and we don't want to go—so we end up just moping about. Or maybe we complain that we're cold because the window is open—then when somebody closes it, we say we're too hot. There's just no pleasing us.

Jesus loved to sit and watch people, especially the children playing, and he knows what tangles we can get ourselves into. It seems that sometimes we don't really know what we *do* want.

But if we follow Jesus, he will make things plain to us. He will help us to sort out the tangles in our lives.

When we get tired...
Matthew 11:25-30

'Come to me, all of you who are tired from carrying heavy loads, and I will give you rest.'
(Verse 28)

There was a tribe of African people who were always busy, dashing here and there doing things. One day a missionary came to live with them and eventually decided to translate the Bible into their language.

All went well until he wanted a word that they didn't have in their language because they were always so busy. The word was 'rest'.

Then one of the tribe came to see him. He'd travelled for many days, he was tired, and thankfully he sank on to a bale of hay. 'I put all my weight on this bale,' he said in his own language. That's it, thought the missionary. 'Put all my weight' means 'rest'.

When we learn to trust Jesus, we can 'put all our weight' on him when we're tired or when we're worried.

DING DONG   DING DONG

I said we shouldn't have nested in the church tower!

A special day
Matthew 12:1-8

'For the Son of Man is Lord of the Sabbath.' (Verse 8)

The Sabbath is the day in the week that's meant to be put aside specially for God. Mostly, it's Sunday, although some people have a Saturday Sabbath.

There are lots of ways of celebrating the Sabbath. The Pharisees invented a long list of rules, partly so that they could disapprove of people who broke them. Some people won't do their washing on the Sabbath; others think that going to church is all that matters.

Jesus is Lord of the Sabbath and he wants us to have what we need, when we need it. (This is not the same as always having what we *want*. Can you tell the difference?) He also wants us to enjoy the Sabbath. But it's a good idea to make this day special by spending some time quietly, thinking about Jesus.

Hands up for Jesus
Matthew 12:9-14

Then Jesus said to the man with the paralysed hand, 'Stretch out your hand.'
(Verse 13)

Stick one hand into your pocket or hold it behind your back and don't use it for a few minutes. Keep on doing the things you normally do. It's not easy, is it? And you certainly can't clap! Try it.

Hands are very important. Grown-ups shake hands to show they want to be friendly. We hold hands with people we love and trust. We 'lend a helping hand' if someone's in difficulty, and we put our hands up in the air to show whose side we're on.

When the man stretched out his hand to Jesus, it was probably the first time he'd been able to use it properly. Jesus had done something wonderful that the man needed.

So it's hands up—who is on the side of Jesus?

Gathering or scattering
Matthew 12:30-32

*'Anyone who is not
for me is really
against me;
anyone who does
not help me gather
is really scattering.'
(Verse 30)*

One of my favourite jobs in autumn is gathering up fallen leaves—sweeping them into a big bright pile. They're such lovely colours all together. They make a chattering noise as I sweep, and they smell good, of earth and things that have grown. When I've finished, I lean on my brush and feel pleased. They'll go on the compost heap, feed the garden and help things to grow.

Sometimes, somebody comes along in a pair of wellies and sets into my lovely pile of leaves, scattering them all over and throwing them into the air, just for fun.

Jesus wants to gather everyone close to himself to love and look after them. By the way we behave, are we helping in this gathering—or are people being scattered in other directions because we're bad advertisements for him?

Matthew 11:16—12:32

Things to do

Giving Jesus a hand

Look at your hand. It's special because it can be used by Jesus. He has no hands but our hands, so think of things your hand can do to help do good to others for him.

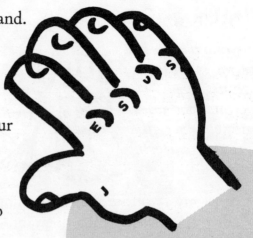

If it helps, you could write the letters J-e-s-u-s, very small, on your knuckles with a ballpoint pen!

Toby + Trish Look, no hands

I could do with a hand with the kitchen floor. Well, as it's Boomerang who made the mess, I'll settle for a paw!

Back to Jonah
Matthew 12:33-41

'On Judgment Day the people of Nineveh will stand up and accuse you, because they turned from their sins when they heard Jonah preach; and I tell you that there is something here greater than Jonah!' (Verse 41)

Have you ever stood in front of one of those bendy mirrors in fun-fairs, that make you look out of shape? The Pharisees were like that. Everything Jesus said, or did, they twisted out of shape. Then they demanded a miracle to try to catch him out. 'Wait,' said Jesus. 'Look at Jonah.'

Jonah was an Old Testament prophet who was very stubborn. 'Go to Nineveh,' said God. So Jonah went the opposite way. He had lots of adventures, including spending three dark days and nights inside a big fish.

Then Jonah went to Nineveh and the people listened to him, recognized the truth and mended their ways. But the Pharisees were worse than the people of Nineveh. They couldn't, or wouldn't, recognize the truth, even from Jesus himself. (Can you see in today's verses why Jesus mentions Jonah?)

42

Happy family
Matthew 12:46-50

'Whoever does what my Father in heaven wants him to do is my brother, my sister, and my mother.' (Verse 50)

Question: Here are two gorgeous, jammy, squidgy cream cakes. One has to be cut into eight, a piece each for the Jones family. The other has to be cut into four, a piece each for the Parker family. Which family would you rather be in? Me, I'd choose the Parker family: with fewer of us, I'd get a bigger piece. I like squidgy cream cake.

Usually, the fewer there are in a share-out, the better for you it is. But this is not so with the love of Jesus. If he loves more people, that doesn't mean he loves each one less. He loves us all the same—completely.

He doesn't love his mother and brothers any less because he loves you and me. We are all his family, and he loves each one of us—completely.

Ground force
Matthew 13:1-9

'But some seeds fell in good soil, and the plants produced corn; some produced a hundred grains, others sixty, and others thirty.' (Verse 8)

There's a programme on television called 'Ground Force', where a group of gardening experts are asked to transform somebody's garden. Large or small, the size doesn't matter. Often it's done as a surprise for somebody who lives in the house and is away.

To begin with, the gardens are either empty and boring or overgrown with weeds. Then 'Ground Force' moves in. They clear away rubbish and weeds, dig flower-beds, and make paths, ponds and patios. Then they plant trees, bushes and flowers.

What a difference! It's the same place, same size, but now it's full of life. The right things are growing there.

When we ask Jesus to move into our life he will transform it and make it bright. Jesus is our 'Ground Force' and we will grow as we were meant to grow.

Look and listen

Matthew
13:10-13

'The reason I use parables in talking to them is that they look, but do not see, and they listen, but do not hear or understand.' (Verse 13)

If you've got something new and important to learn, it helps you to understand it if you have something to look at.

There was once a man called Jeremiah. He had a message from God for the people of Jerusalem and thereabouts. They had been so wicked that God was going to destroy them and their city. It would be impossible to put themselves together again. Jeremiah picked up a large clay pot and dropped it. Crash!! The people of Jerusalem looked very surprised, but they knew exactly what Jeremiah meant.

Jesus' message was so new and important, so exciting, that it wasn't always easy to understand at first. So he used parables, or word-pictures, about things they already knew. 'Look at that man sowing his seed. See what happens to it. Why?' Then they could understand.

What's it all about?
Matthew 13:18-23

'And the seeds sown in the good soil stand for those who hear the message and understand it.'
(Verse 23a)

It's all about you and me and Jesus. The 'seeds' are the words of Jesus, and we are where the seeds land.

The seeds that land on the *hard path* don't stand a chance. Soon it's as if they'd never been there. Finished.

The seeds on the *rocks* make a feeble start. We may even love Jesus for a while. Then we meet people who don't love Jesus and things get difficult. Finished.

The *prickly and weedy* patches really want the seeds at first. But there's so much else there already. Things we must do, places to go, things to get, worries. There's no time, amongst it all, for Jesus. Finished.

But there's another way. If we're *good soil*, and really listen to the words of Jesus and want to put him first, then we'll grow closer to him each day.

Things to do

God's seeds

Here is a seed packet showing all the produce (the Bible calls it fruit) that comes from good soil.

Colour in the picture, making the flowers really bright and colourful, the vegetables fresh and crisp and the fruit mouth-watering and juicy! Then think how you too are part of God's beautiful garden produce.

Toby + Trish — Seeds of unrest

Am I worth it?

It's worth it
Matthew 13:31–34 and 45–46

'Also, the Kingdom of heaven is like this. A man is looking for fine pearls, and when he finds one that is unusually fine, he goes and sells everything that he has, and buys that pearl.' (Verses 45–46)

Just imagine that your friend's dog has had puppies and you go to visit. One puppy in particular catches your eye. You look at him—he looks at you—and you just have to have him. But Mum can't afford to buy a puppy. 'You can have him if you give up your spending money until he's paid for,' she says. No more trips to the swimming baths, no more sweets or computer games. 'When you've got him, he'll have to be taken for walks, brushed and fed,' says Mum wisely.

You have to think hard. Then, 'Right. Let's get him. He'll be worth it,' you say. And he is—all the fun and the friendship. And when he's grown up, he'll warn you of danger.

God's kingdom is like that, but sometimes it's necessary to give up things for Jesus. If we do, it will be worth it.

They didn't know him
Matthew 13:53-58

'Isn't he the carpenter's son? ... Where did he get all this?'... And so they rejected him. (Verses 55, 56, 57)

NAZARETH JOINERY
Proprietors
Joseph and sons

Do you know:

♦ How many windows there are in your classroom?
♦ What colour the ceiling is?
♦ What things are fastened on the walls?

Sometimes we know a place, or a person, so well that we don't really see them any more. It's a good idea to look at someone you know as if you've just met them. You'll be surprised.

Jesus had been brought up in Nazareth. People were so used to seeing him around that they didn't see him as he really was. To them, he was just part of Mary and Joseph's family.

And because they couldn't see him as he really was, Jesus wasn't able to work among them.

Perhaps we, too, should take a new look at Jesus—as if we'd just met him. Then we'll know who he really is.

Herod on the fence
Matthew 14:1-12

Herod wanted to kill John the Baptist, but he was afraid of the Jewish people, because they considered John to be a prophet. (Verse 5)

Sometimes you have a decision to make and you don't know what to do. So you dither about and do nothing. We call it 'sitting on the fence' (another word-picture). Sitting on a fence can be very uncomfortable!

Herod was feeling uncomfortable. He'd put John in prison because John had had the cheek to criticize Herod's marriage and his wife. His wife was angry and wanted John killed. But if he killed John, the Jewish people would be angry. So there he was, sitting on his fence. In the end he was tricked into having John killed.

If we have a decision to make, it's best to think it out carefully, maybe ask advice, pray about it, then do what we feel is right. If we 'sit on the fence' we're not really solving anything.

Enough to go round
Matthew 14:13-21

'All we have here are five loaves and two fish,' the disciples replied. 'Then bring them here to me,' Jesus said. (Verses 17–18)

Could it have been that the disciples were hungry themselves? After all, they'd been with Jesus and the crowds all day. 'Send them away to find food,' they said. 'It's nothing to do with us. There's not even enough food for us.' They were still disciples wearing 'L' plates.

Jesus must have been hungry and tired himself. But he wouldn't let the people go until he'd seen that they had what they needed. 'Give them something to eat yourselves,' he said. Jesus knew that the disciples couldn't do this. But what they could do was to forget how hungry they themselves were and bring what food they had to Jesus. Then he could make it into something wonderful.

This was a picnic everyone would always remember!

Peter walks on water
Matthew 14:22-33

At once Jesus reached out and grabbed hold of Peter and said, 'How little faith you have! Why did you doubt?' (Verse 31)

Have you ever tried to skim flat pebbles over water? You count how many times they bounce. It's fun. It's also difficult because you need lots of strength to do it properly. Eventually the pebble always sinks beneath the water.

This story about Peter walking on the water is only told in Matthew's Gospel. Peter was always doing things without thinking about what would happen as a result. When he became wiser, and lost his 'L' plate, it was his courage that made him such a great disciple.

Matthew tells us this story for a reason. We can't, we mustn't, even *think* of walking on water. Just like that pebble, we would sink. But if we're troubled, and things are crashing around us, we can reach out in our hearts to Jesus, and he will hold us.

Things to do

Baskets of leftovers

Here's how you can make a super little basket to remind you of the story of the mammoth picnic.

You need a 10 cm disc of corrugated cardboard, ten cocktail sticks and some 5 mm strips of coloured paper. Ask a grown-up to help you to cut the sticks in half and stick the pointed ends into the cardboard as shown in the diagram. Then 'weave' the paper in and out of the sticks. When you get to the second layer, weave it *out and in* to make the basket. When it's finished, collect up some breadcrumbs and thank Jesus for all your food—then throw the crumbs to the birds.

Toby + Trish — Crumbs

I like shaking the cloth after tea...

...I feed the birds with the crumbs...

...and, if it takes long enough, I miss the washing-up!

We've always done it this way
Matthew 15:1-9

'It is no use for them to worship me, because they teach human rules as though they were my laws!'
(Verse 9)

Imagine that you're living a long time ago. What's it like getting up on a cold, dark winter's morning? No lights, no central heating, no hot water. Chattering teeth! It's freezing. Downstairs Mum's cooking breakfast over a fire by the light of an oil lamp. No television. No computers.

Then a young man knocks at the door. 'I've come to connect you up,' he says, 'to a new power called electricity.' 'We don't need any new power,' says Mum. 'We've always done it this way.' And she slams the door. What would you think?

The Pharisees were all tied up in old ways and old rules. Some of them meant nothing. Jesus was offering them new ways, with a power to change their lives. But... 'We've always done it this way,' they said.

Clean inside
Matthew 15:10-20

'But the things that come out of the mouth come from the heart, and these are the things that make a person ritually unclean.'
(Verse 18)

I have a beautiful jam pan. It's huge, it's heavy, and it's made out of brass. Mostly it sits in a corner and twinkles at me, but sometimes it goes dull. I sigh, get out my metal polish and dusters and give it a good clean. There—it's twinkling at me again.

But it's not really of any use. Even though it looks good, it's not really clean. If I made jam in it, it would taste nasty—of metal polish.

Jesus is not really concerned with how clean we are on the *outside*, where it shows. It's our *inside* where we do our thinking and feeling that interests him. We may twinkle on the *outside* but if our *inside* isn't really clean, everything we do or say will turn nasty. We'll be of no use to Jesus.

A test of faith
Matthew 15:21–31

Jesus answered her, 'You are a woman of great faith! What you want will be done for you.' (Verse 28)

'We've always done it this way.' 'We've always behaved this way.' They're both as bad.

When Jesus went into Canaan, it was the only time we know of, during his work, that he left his own country of Palestine. And the people of Canaan and the people of Palestine had always behaved in an unfriendly way towards each other. It took courage, therefore, for the Canaanite woman to come to Jesus and ask him a big favour. Jesus had to test her to make sure she meant what she said. So he ignored her plea for help.

Her Canaanite pride had gone. She was willing to accept whatever Jesus would do. 'Help me,' she said.

Because of her great faith, Jesus was able to cross the division between the Jewish people and the Canaanites and perform a special miracle. He healed the woman's daughter without even seeing her.

A hungry crowd
Matthew 15:32-39

They all ate and had enough. Then the disciples took up seven baskets full of pieces left over. (Verse 37)

One of my favourite fairy stories is 'The Magic Porridge Pot'. A poor little girl goes into the forest collecting sticks for the fire. There she meets a frail old lady and, feeling sorry for her, shares her lunch, a crust of bread, with her.

In return, the old lady gives her a magic porridge pot. 'Just say, "Cook, pot, cook" and you'll have as much porridge as you need. You'll never be hungry again.' The story goes on, but that's the best bit.

Jesus knows that our bodies need food, and Matthew is telling us another story about how Jesus looks after people who are hungry.

In John's Gospel, chapter 6 verse 35, Jesus calls himself 'the bread of life'. He is what we need if we are to live as God wants us to.

That yeast again
Matthew 16:5-12

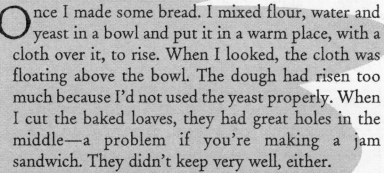

Then the disciples understood that he was not warning them to guard themselves from the yeast used in bread but from the teaching of the Pharisees and Sadducees. (Verse 12)

Once I made some bread. I mixed flour, water and yeast in a bowl and put it in a warm place, with a cloth over it, to rise. When I looked, the cloth was floating above the bowl. The dough had risen too much because I'd not used the yeast properly. When I cut the baked loaves, they had great holes in the middle—a problem if you're making a jam sandwich. They didn't keep very well, either.

Jesus is speaking in word pictures again to help his disciples understand his teaching. Yeast can sometimes be a problem. The Pharisees were all puffed up with their big ideas, like my dough. But they had nothing important or lasting to say. Inside they were empty, full of holes, like my loaves.

Matthew 15:1—16:12

Things to do

Bread of life

In the Bible, 'bread' means 'food', because that was what people depended on in that country. They didn't make sandwiches, they just broke off big chunks and dipped them into their meal.

See how many different foods you can think of that people in other countries depend on as their daily 'bread'. Draw the things you think of in the boxes.

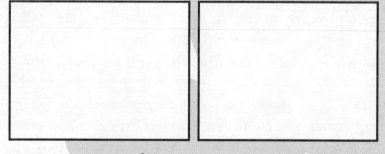

Toby + Trish — Spag bog

No wonder they're always tied up when I need a walk—they're eating string!

Peter sees daylight
Matthew 16:13-20

Simon Peter answered, 'You are the Messiah, the Son of the living God.' (Verse 16)

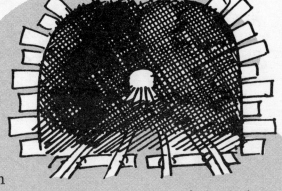

Travelling on a steam train is fun—until it plunges into a tunnel. If the lights don't go on—and they don't always—there you are, more or less in the dark. You can't be sure who's who, and what's what. It's very confusing. Then suddenly you're out in the daylight. You can see things clearly.

No wonder Peter had been feeling confused and a bit in the dark. So much had happened since he'd followed Jesus that he wasn't sure what was what any more. Then, suddenly, it was just as if he'd shot out into the daylight. Things that Jesus had said and done made sense. Peter knew, without any doubt, that Jesus was God's chosen one, God's own Son.

No turning back
Matthew 16:21-28

Jesus turned around and said to Peter, 'Get away from me, Satan! You are an obstacle in my way, because these thoughts of yours don't come from God, but from human nature.' (Verse 23)

Poor Peter. He must have felt like a yo-yo... up and down, up and down. Jesus had been so pleased with him when he'd said who Jesus was. Now he was accusing Peter of getting in the way of God's plans. Up and down, up and down.

Following Jesus is not always easy. We have to make decisions and choices. Often we're tempted to take the easy way out. An easy way out for Jesus would have been to turn around and walk away from Jerusalem and what would happen there, as Peter wanted him to. Maybe he would have saved his own life, but that wasn't God's plan.

Following Jesus means doing what *he* wants, not what *we* want—not what *I* want. When we cross out our 'I', what do we get? The shape of the cross of Jesus.

The high point
Matthew 17:1-9

While he was talking, a shining cloud came over them, and a voice from the cloud said, 'This is my own dear Son, with whom I am pleased—listen to him!' (Verse 5)

There's a story about a famous king of England called Henry the Fifth. It was the evening before he was to lead his soldiers at the battle of Agincourt. Henry knew that they would be anxious about what was going to happen and would need encouragement. So he took off his crown, put on an old cloak, and went round among them, talking to them. He became one of them.

The next morning, they saw this same man in all his kingly armour, sitting on his magnificent horse. They knew that their friend of the night before was also their king. They won the battle.

Jesus wanted his disciples to know him not just as their friend but as their king before they faced the difficult times ahead.

With God's help
Matthew 17:14-20

'It was because you haven't enough faith,' answered Jesus. *'I assure you* that if you have faith as big as a mustard seed, you can say to this hill, "Go from here to there!" and it will go. You could do anything!' (Verse 20)

> I think I'll move my bedroom around... TOBY!!

I was watching a very little boy playing in his garden. His bricks were spread all over the grass but he decided he wanted to build on the patio. So he collected his bricks and put them in their box. Well done! Then he found he couldn't lift it—it was too heavy. He pulled and tugged until his face was like a beetroot.

'Daddy!' he called, and together they heaved the box of bricks on to the patio. Then they settled down together to build a lovely castle.

We may know what we want to do for Jesus but it's no use trying to do it on our own. We need to ask God's help, in faith. Then together we can do things that wouldn't be possible for us to do on our own.

Whose house is it, anyway?
Matthew 17:24-27

'But we don't want to offend these people. So go to the lake and drop in a line. Pull up the first fish you hook, and in its mouth you will find a coin worth enough for my temple tax and yours. Take it and pay them our taxes.' (Verse 27)

Sometimes during school holidays, or at weekends, it's fun to visit large houses where famous people have lived. The houses are usually very old and full of beautiful furniture and paintings. Just fancy having your cornflakes in a room that size!

(Next day) Now my bedroom's all tidy, you've got to pay to come in!

Outside, you can wander round the gardens, picnic, and sometimes play giant games of snakes and ladders or hopscotch. The only problem is, you have to pay to go in because the house doesn't belong to you.

It was a bit of a cheek for the authorities to expect Jesus to pay the temple tax when the temple belonged to God, and therefore to Jesus himself. But just to avoid another argument with the Pharisees about something that wasn't all that important, Jesus paid his taxes. God himself provided the money.

75

Matthew 16:13—17:27

Things to do

Going up

Sitting on top of a mountain and looking down at the world is one of the best feelings you can have. It's so much easier to think clearly up there. And if it's good for us, think how much more important it must have been for people when Matthew's amazing book was written—that was the highest they could get!

Colour this picture of a mountain, a hot-air balloon, a jumbo jet and a satellite in space. That's how high we can get now!

Toby + Trish — Coming down

I can see from here that those windows are streaky!

The greatest
Matthew 18:1-7

I can't imagine I'll get anything worth having from Trish—but you never know...

'The greatest in the Kingdom of heaven is the one who humbles himself and becomes like this child.' (Verse 4)

Of course, everybody knows that children can be little horrors! But, on the other hand, they're special.

When my children were small, always at the end of their Christmas present list they wrote 'A surprise'. They loved surprises—I'm sure *you* do. 'Close your eyes and hold out your hand,' someone says to you. And you screw up your eyes and stand on tiptoe, wondering what the surprise will be.

Sadly, as we get older, we don't seem to have time for surprises. Life has a 'sameness' and we're tangled up with worries instead. We plan our time so that every minute is organized—and we leave no room for God to step in.

But our God is a God of surprises. He has wonderful things planned for us in his wonderful world. Let's keep on our toes and be ready for them. Always!

77

Mountain rescue
Matthew 18:10–14
and 19–20

'In just the same way your Father in heaven does not want any of these little ones to be lost.' (Verse 14)

We were on holiday in the Lake District in northern England. It's lovely there. The mountains are the highest in England. Every morning, people set off in big heavy boots, with big heavy rucksacks, to climb them.

One night there was a commotion in front of our hotel—flashing lights, cars, people wearing helmets. It was the 'Mountain Rescue' team. A walker had set off, but he hadn't come back. He'd broken the rules: he'd gone alone and he hadn't told anyone where he was going.

All night they searched. In the morning they found him—cold, hungry, in pain with a broken leg. They saved his life.

Jesus is our 'Mountain Rescue'. We break the rules, and end up in a mess, but he always comes looking for us.

God's forgiveness
Matthew 18:21-35

*'So he called the servant in. "You worthless slave!"
he said. "I forgave you the whole amount you
owed me, just because you asked me to. You
should have had mercy on your fellow servant,
just as I had mercy on you."'* (Verses 32–33)

Millions of pounds! That's an awful lot of money. I
wonder what the servant had been doing to spend
all that much? Maybe he'd gone camel-racing. You
can lose a whole heap of money camel-racing if you
pick the slow ones. Whatever… he was found out.

Lucky for him that he had such a kind and loving
master. Pity for him that some of this kindness and
love didn't rub off on him.

God knows exactly what we've been up to—
disliking people, not being honest… there's more!
But he loves us, and when we're
truly sorry for what we've done,
and tell him so, he'll
forgive us. Let's
make sure that
some of God's love rubs
off on us, like pollen from a
flower. Then we'll become kind
and loving too.

It's impossible
Matthew 19:1-11

'So they are no longer two, but one. No human being must separate, then, what God has joined together.'
(Verse 6)

THROUGH JESUS

In the beginning, when God made the world and everything in it, it was very beautiful. It still is. Spring, summer, autumn, winter—they're all beautiful. Which is your favourite season? Why?

Sadly, we cut ourselves loose from God and some things went wrong. Sometimes, even love goes wrong. God knows all about this. He knows how, no matter how hard we and grown-ups try, things don't always work out as we want them to.

God sent us perfect love—he sent us Jesus. Through Jesus we can be joined up once more with God. In the same way, when a man and a woman fall in love, God wants them to be truly joined together for keeps, through Jesus.

It is still possible for love to be as it was in the beginning.

Come as you are
Matthew 19:13–15

Jesus said, 'Let the children come to me and do not stop them, because the Kingdom of heaven belongs to such as these.' (Verse 14)

You'll know all about time warps and space travel? Right. Here we go. Just come as you are.

We're in Palestine, nearly two thousand years ago. It's hot, and it's dusty. A man is sitting in the middle of a crowd of people. He wears loose robes, his face is light brown, with a beard, and he looks very tired.

Other children are walking towards this man—Chinese, Indian, French—from every country. They've come as they are. He smiles at us, and his smile says, 'Welcome.' His face is full of love. Some men near him try to stop us—but he holds out his arms to us.

As we gather round him, we feel his hand on our head, each one. It's good to be together with Jesus. Jesus, Lord of the time warp.

81

Matthew 18:1—19:15

Things to do

Find the lost sheep

Here's some fun for you and your friends. Draw a picture of a sheep on thin card. Colour it in and cut it out with a little folded flap underneath so that it stands up.

Send somebody out of the room and hide the sheep somewhere. When they come back in, you all sing or say, 'How green you are, how green you are...' very quietly if they are nowhere near the sheep, and very loudly if they come close to it. Shout at the top of your voices just before they touch it!

Right about turn
Matthew 19:16-30

'But many who now are first will be last, and many who now are last will be first.' (Verse 30)

When my husband was in the army, he had to march a squad of soldiers to the canteen every day for their dinner. He noticed that the same soldiers were always in the front line and so got their dinner first. So... one day he marched the squad *past* the canteen. Then, 'Right about turn,' he shouted. The back row became the front row and they got their dinner first.

Following Jesus can sometimes turn our lives back to front. We think we're doing all right really... then, 'Right about turn,' says Jesus, and we realize we're not.

To follow Jesus, we need to put him first, before anything else. The rich man loved Jesus, but he loved his money more. And oh dear, pity that poor camel!

Don't keep looking sideways
Matthew 20:1-16

'Listen, friend,' the owner answered one of them, 'I have not cheated you. After all, you agreed to do a day's work for one silver coin.'
(Verse 13)

When my three children were small, serving out at mealtimes was difficult sometimes. Three pairs of eyes watched every spoonful—potatoes, stew, vegetables—as it landed on each plate. Then three pairs of eyes followed each plate on its journey across the table until it landed in front of one of them. They were making sure brother or sister didn't get more than they did. One day we had to count the peas!

If we're not careful, as we get older this sort of thing becomes a habit. 'Are they getting more than I am? Am I being cheated?' What a sad waste of time.

God loves you as if there was nobody else in the world—and he loves your friend in just the same way, so we don't need to keep looking sideways.

Through thick and thin
Matthew 20:17–28

'What do you want?' Jesus asked her. She answered, 'Promise me that these two sons of mine will sit on your right and your left when you are King.' 'You don't know what you are asking for,' Jesus answered the sons. 'Can you drink the cup of suffering that I am about to drink?' (Verses 21–22)

Isn't that just like a mum—wanting the best for her children? Even though James and John were grown men, they were still her children.

Jesus was preparing his disciples for what was going to happen in Jerusalem. They'd understood the 'king' bit and felt that, as Jesus' friends, they should be there at the 'top table'. They were a bit hazy about what Jesus' kingdom actually was.

And what about the suffering and the sadness first? The disciples couldn't, or wouldn't, understand this. Like small children, they'd gone for the cherry on top of the bun and ignored the rest.

Being Jesus' friend is not just for the good times. He wants us to stick by him in the hard times, too—through thick and thin.

How do you see?
Matthew 20:29-34

*Jesus had pity on the
two blind men and
touched their eyes;
at once they were
able to see, and they
followed him. (Verse 34)*

See ya!

A while ago, I was working in a day centre for blind people. On my second visit, as I walked into the room, a young lady called Elizabeth said, 'Hi, Peggy.' Elizabeth couldn't see at all. 'How did you know it was me?' I asked. 'By the sound of your footsteps,' she said. Her ears told her what her eyes couldn't.

The blind men couldn't see at all. But when they heard Jesus' footsteps among all that crowd, they knew immediately who he was. 'Jesus, Son of David'—God's chosen one. They knew in their hearts what their eyes couldn't tell them.

Sometimes we have our eyes wide open, but we don't see things properly. If we close our eyes, we can come close to Jesus and know things as they really are.

Who is he?
Matthew 21:1-11

WELCOME—whoever you are!

When Jesus entered Jerusalem, the whole city was thrown into an uproar. 'Who is he?' the people asked. (Verse 10)

I'm a nosey parker. If there's a crowd collecting to watch something, I join them to see what they're watching. You could have fun 'crowd collecting' in the park or schoolyard. Pretend you're watching something, hard, and see how long it takes for your friends to start looking too.

The crowd gathering in Jerusalem had something special to watch. A young man riding on a donkey, like a king travelling in peace. Coats were thrown on the ground, branches cut off trees. I'd certainly have run to see what was going on. I bet you would too.

'Who is he?' they asked. Was 'the prophet Jesus, from Nazareth in Galilee' the right answer? We know it wasn't. Jesus was much, much more than that. The people of Jerusalem had no idea just who it was they'd given such a wonderful welcome to.

Matthew 19:16—21:11

Things to do

Up periscope

If you had been standing at the back of the Palm Sunday crowd, you wouldn't have been able to see Jesus on that wonderful day. You would have needed a periscope!

Ask a grown-up if you can borrow two small mirrors and hold them as shown in the picture, so that you can look through the top mirror by looking at the bottom one. You will be able to see on the tops of cupboards and over doors!

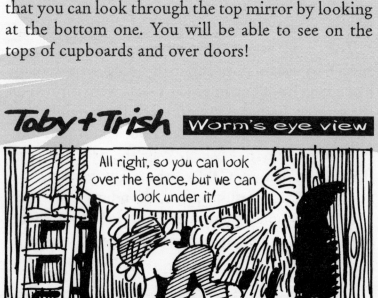

Toby + Trish — Worm's eye view

All right, so you can look over the fence, but we can look under it!

Spring cleaning at the temple
Matthew 21:12-17

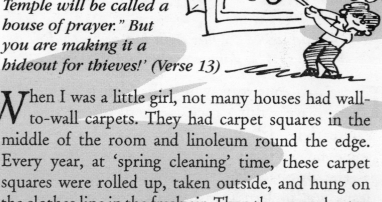

Jesus said to them, 'It is written in the Scriptures that God said, "My Temple will be called a house of prayer." But you are making it a hideout for thieves!' (Verse 13)

When I was a little girl, not many houses had wall-to-wall carpets. They had carpet squares in the middle of the room and linoleum round the edge. Every year, at 'spring cleaning' time, these carpet squares were rolled up, taken outside, and hung on the clothes line in the fresh air. Then they were beaten with cane beaters—whack! whack!—until every speck of dirt had been thrashed out of them. I was allowed my 'whack' and I really punished those carpets.

Jesus didn't often get angry. But he couldn't bear to see his Father's house, the temple, being used in the wrong ways, even dishonest ways.

So he 'spring cleaned' the temple. He got rid of the 'dirt', those things that shouldn't have been there, and made it clean and fresh and lovely again.

Who do you think you are?
Matthew 21:18-27

Jesus came back to the Temple; and as he taught, the chief priests and the elders came to him and asked, 'What right have you to do these things? Who gave you this right?' (Verse 23)

There's an American saying: 'between a rock and a hard place'. 'But a rock *is* a hard place,' you say. Quite right. It's just a clever way of saying that someone's in trouble and there's no way out.

The priests and elders were getting desperate. Jesus was in Jerusalem causing a stir wherever he went. They had to get rid of him. So here they are, trying to trick him into the crime of speaking against God, punishable by death. 'Who do you think you are?' they asked. If he said he was God, they had him.

They were clever men, but Jesus was cleverer. Instead of answering their question, he asked *them* one—like a game of ping-pong. Whatever they answered, they were the ones in trouble now. They were between a rock and a hard place.

Mean what you say
Matthew 21:28–31a

'Which one of the two did what his father wanted?'
(Verse 31a)

Washing-up or football?

Are you a 'doer' or a 'say-you'll-doer?' They're different.

One day, a teacher mentioned in class that old Mrs Pringle down the road wasn't feeling well. 'It would be nice if somebody did her shopping.' Sarah's hand shot up. 'I'll go, Miss, after school,' she said. The teacher smiled at her, and the rest of the class shuffled, especially Mick, who wanted to go to rugby practice after school.

As Mick passed on his way to rugby practice, he saw Mrs Pringle sitting by her window, waiting. On his way back, she was still waiting. So Mick did her shopping.

The Pharisees, whom Jesus was talking to in today's reading, were 'say-you'll-doers'. Their mouths said the right things but nothing happened.

Lord Jesus, help me to be a 'doer', not a 'say-you'll-doer'.

How do you spell it?

V-i-n-y-a-r-d?

Vineyard quiz
Matthew 21:33-45

'And so I tell you,' added Jesus, *'the Kingdom of God will be taken away from you and given to a people who will produce the proper fruits.'* (Verse 43)

Jesus told his parables for a reason. Here's a quiz to find out what he meant with this one, which he told to the Pharisees. You'll need your Bible with you to find the answers.

1. Who was the owner of the vineyard?
2. What was the vineyard?
3. Why did the tenants behave so badly?
4. Who were the slaves that the owner sent to the vineyard?
5. Who was the owner's son?
6. What two words might describe how the owner behaved up to verse 39?
7. In verse 43, who are 'the people who will produce the proper fruit'?

Answers: 1. God. 2. The world. 3. They thought the vineyard belonged to them. 4. The Old Testament prophets. 5. Jesus himself. 6. Patient, loving (you may have others). 7. Everyone who loves Jesus.

Will you come?
Matthew 22:1-10

So the servants went out into the streets and gathered all the people they could find, good and bad alike; and the wedding hall was filled with people. (Verse 10)

Sometimes you pass a house with a great bunch of balloons tied to the gate and you know there's a party going on there. If you're like me, you love parties, and you feel a bit envious that you weren't invited. You want to get in there and join in the fun.

So what sort of people turn down an invitation to a party—especially a king's party? Maybe they don't want anything to do with the king; maybe they don't believe he's really a king; maybe they're so busy with their own affairs that they've no time for anything else. They don't know what they're missing!

God is the king of heaven and earth and we're all invited to share the wonderful things he has for us. We can't turn down an invitation like that.

93

Matthew 21:12—22:10

Things to do

Was it a good party?

Suppose that instead of inviting all your friends to your next party (and the children who had invited you to theirs!) you could ask *anybody* in the whole world to come. Who would you ask?

You could ask your favourite pop star, but also people who would really enjoy coming because they never get asked to parties.

Toby + Trish — Last gasp

It's going to be a quiet party!

Bad manners
Matthew 22:11–14

'Friend, how did you get in here without wedding clothes?' the king asked him. But the man said nothing. (Verse 12)

On a holiday in Greece, we visited Mystra, an ancient city over eight hundred years old. There are ruined houses and palaces, lovely churches, and a monastery where the nuns still live.

They welcome you with smiles but insist you enter their special place suitably dressed—no shorts or scanty sunwear. At the gates are rails of skirts, blouses, shirts and baggy trousers for you to pop on over the top. Because you are their guests, it would be bad-mannered and thoughtless to go against the wishes of the nuns.

At weddings in Palestine, special wedding garments were provided by the host for each guest to wear. By not wearing his, and not even answering the king, the man was very bad-mannered. He didn't really want to be part of the celebrations, and deserved to be thrown out.

95

Either... or?
Matthew 22:15-22

So Jesus said to them, 'Well, then, pay the Emperor what belongs to the Emperor, and pay God what belongs to God.' (Verse 21)

There go those Pharisees again. They must have spent all their time huddled together thinking up questions to catch Jesus out.

Palestine was ruled by the Romans. Should the Jewish people *either* obey Roman laws, like paying taxes to Rome, *or* worship God? Jesus' answer could *either* offend the Romans *or* offend the Jewish people. But it's not a question of *either/or*. Jesus made it clear that laws must be obeyed, however hard that is. We must be part of what is happening around us. *And* God can also be worshipped, because he is the God of everyday things.

Sometimes we try to separate things out, but God will not be separated. He is not either/or. God is *everything*.

In the centre
Matthew 22:34-40

Jesus answered, 'Love the Lord your God with all your heart, with all your soul, and with all your mind.' (Verse 37)

I used to make pottery... not very well, but it was fun. The clay had to be soft and gungy, but not too soft and gungy. Turning the wheel with my foot treadle, at just the right moment, I flung on to it a lump of clay. Then came the exciting bit. Working the clay with fingers and thumbs, I hollowed it and drew it upwards. I was making a large vase... wobble, wobble. No, a small vase... wobble, wobble. Well, a little jar... wobble, wobble, wobble. Ah well, here comes another pepper pot. The important thing was to get the clay right in the centre of the wheel, which I could never do.

If God is not right in the centre of our loving, our thinking and our feeling, our lives will be just one wobble after another... worth no more than a pepper pot. And full of holes!

All talk
Matthew 23:1–12

'They do everything so that people will see them.'
(Verse 5a)

It's nice to be the centre of attention just for a while. Maybe you've won the hundred metres in the school sports; your friends gather round and pat your shoulder. Then everybody claps as you receive a cup. Or maybe you've broken your arm and it's in plaster; your friends tap on it, and write on it, and ask how you are.

But the Pharisees enjoyed being the centre of attention *all* the time—strutting about in special gear, having the best seats at parties. Yet at bedtime, when they took off their fancy Pharisees' outfits and got into their nightshirts, they were nothing—just like empty jars.

There's a saying: 'You can talk the talk, but can you walk the walk?' The Pharisees were all talk.

Safe and warm
Matthew 23:37-39 and 24:1-2

'Jerusalem, Jerusalem! You kill the prophets and stone the messengers God has sent you! How many times have I wanted to put my arms round all your people, just as a hen gathers her chicks under her wings, but you would not let me!' (Verse 37)

We were watching some new chickens—twelve balls of yellow fluff on matchstick legs. They were lovely. Then, unfortunately, we got too close. Immediately mother hen called them and they scuttled, flapping tiny wings, and disappeared underneath her... all twelve! They were safe and warm and snug. Mother hen fixed us with her beady eyes: 'Not another step!'

Time and again, God had sent his prophets to the Jewish people, warning them of troubles to come, but did they listen? They did not. They laughed, then stoned and killed God's messengers. Now Jesus himself had come, and they still wouldn't be warned.

Jesus is calling us to himself—safe in the warmth of his love, where nothing can really hurt us.

Matthew 22:11—24:2

Things to do

God in the centre

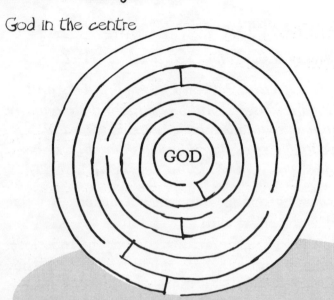

Can you find your way to the centre of this maze? You'll sometimes go the wrong way and have to find your way back—just as in real life!

You could make a maze of your own. Any size, as long as you put God in the centre.

Toby + Trish — Off target

Why don't you shut your eyes when you throw? The rest of us do!

When the going gets tough
Matthew 24:3-14

'But whoever holds out to the end will be saved.'
(Verse 13)

There's a lovely painting called 'Peace'. Can you guess what it's about? It's not a garden full of flowers, or a beautiful sunset. It's not a baby fast asleep, or anything like these.

It's a painting of a storm at sea. The wind is whipping the waves into great peaks and they're dashing over sharp rocks and pounding against high cliffs. You can almost hear the noise. Funny sort of peace, that?

On the cliff top is a little tree, bending over the edge in the wind. In its branches is a nest, and in that nest a bird is sitting on its eggs. That's peace.

Sometimes, things happen around us that we don't understand. We feel tossed about and worried. But if we hold on to Jesus, we will come through safely. We will feel his peace inside us.

Gosh!

He will come again
Matthew 24:29-31

'Then the sign of the Son of Man will appear in the sky; and all the peoples of earth will weep as they see the Son of Man coming on the clouds of heaven with power and great glory.'
(Verse 30)

There are lots of things we take for granted. They've always been there and we can't imagine life without them. Because we live where we do, we know there'll always be food when we're hungry, and a cosy bed when we're tired. But some children in different parts of the world have learned to take nothing for granted. Their lives have been ruined by wars.

On caravan holidays when my children were younger, we used to 'star-watch'. We took it for granted that the 'Plough' and 'Orion's belt' would be where they'd always been at that time of the year.

Jesus warns us not to take anything for granted. Things change. Even the stars might fall. Only one thing is certain: he will come again, as Lord, and everything that is wrong will be put right.

Yesterday, today and for ever
Matthew 24:32-35

'Heaven and earth will pass away, but my words will never pass away.' (Verse 35)

Auntie Hilda is an impor-tant member of our family. She's a great big teddy bear. She came to us one Christmas when my daughter was fifteen months old. Melanie is now thirty-four, so Auntie Hilda is quite old for a bear.

She sits upright, with her legs spread always in front of her. She's been cuddled and sat on, dragged by her ears and turned upside down. Now she's falling apart. We've done our best to make her last— we've stitched and patched her. Now there's not much left to patch. She won't last for ever. Nothing does... except Jesus, who is the living word of God. John starts *his* Gospel by saying that Jesus was there at the beginning. But he's also with us now. And, as we saw in our last reading, he will be there at the end of the world.

Ready!
Matthew 24:36-44

Next show 6 years, 11 months, 30 days and 23 hours!

'So then, you must always be ready, because the Son of Man will come at an hour when you are not expecting him.' (Verse 44)

There's an unusual cactus that only flowers once every seven years. That's difficult enough if you happen to be someone who's interested in cactus and you want to see it flowering. But to make things even more difficult, this flower only lasts a few hours.

Just imagine. You water it and watch it, feed it and maybe sing to it for seven years… then you decide to go for a picnic, or shopping. And when you get back, it's been and gone. How awful! You should have stayed at home.

Nobody knows when Jesus will come again as Lord of the world. We're not meant to know. The important thing is that when he comes, we're ready.

No warning
Matthew 25:1–13

And Jesus concluded,
'Be on your guard, then,
because you do not know
the day or the hour.' (Verse 13)

Next
OFSTED:
Any time!

Usually, when a school inspector pays a visit, everybody knows well in advance. So every-body's on his and her best behaviour. Work is ready to be shown, and everybody listens to the teacher (or looks as though they are). No bad manners. You're the perfect class (or look as though you are).

But what might happen if the inspector turns up without warning? Ahh! Maybe you haven't done your homework because there was something good on television; maybe you feel bad-tempered and are snarling a bit at the person next to you. Maybe somebody's missing who should be there.

When Jesus comes again in glory, there'll be no warning. There won't be a chance to sort ourselves out. Better to know him already, in our hearts... right now.

Things to do

Ready

Make a 3D picture of an 'Ever Ready' battery.

Paint 'EVER READY' in yellow letters on a piece of card 10 cm x 15 cm. Fill in the background in red. Roll the card against the edge of a table when it's dry, to make a battery shape.

Put the curved 'battery' down on another piece of card 15 cm x 20 cm. Cut two slits in the new card where the battery touches. Push the edges of the battery through the slits and secure at the back with glue. Pin it to the wall in your bedroom, or hang it with string, to remind you that Jesus is coming again, soon...

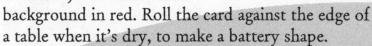

Toby + Trish — Always ready

So you're ready to go out, are you, Boomerang? All I need is my coat, scarf, gloves, wellies and a dog-lead

Nobody like you
Matthew 25:14–30

I doubt if anybody would want to be like me!

'Well done, you good and faithful servant!' said his master. 'You have been faithful in managing small amounts, so I will put you in charge of large amounts. Come on in and share my happiness!' (Verse 21)

It's amazing to think that of all the millions of people in the world, there's nobody just like you—or me. Twins, even triplets, sometimes look alike, but they don't always think and feel alike. And because of who we are, we have special gifts.

We might not be able to swim for miles, or bake a cake, or bungy-jump. We might go to pieces in front of a computer game (I do). But there's always something special that we can do.

Maybe we're good at 'putting ourselves into somebody else's shoes' and understanding how they're feeling. Maybe we have a lovely smile and don't moan about everything. Maybe we find it easier to love than to dislike. First, discover your gifts. Then use them, and see what happens.

87

Do it for me
Matthew 25:31-46

Trish is feeling poorly today, so I've bought her a comic

The King will reply, 'I tell you, whenever you did this for one of the least important of these members of my family, you did it for me!' (Verse 40)

I'm sure you wouldn't be unkind on purpose. You wouldn't want to hurt anybody. But there's a sort of unkindness we don't always think about. We wouldn't want to hurt anybody—but would we want to help if necessary? Or do we pretend that others don't need help, and take no notice?

It's easy to be helpful to those in our own little group, whom we know well. But what about the boy who's just arrived in our class and doesn't know anybody, or the girl we don't like whose mum's in hospital? Being friendly can make a big difference to them.

Jesus has done everything for us. We can show our love for him by helping those who need it. He loves them too. We can do it for him.

The best she had
Matthew 26:1-13

Jesus knew what they were saying, so he said to them, 'Why are you bothering this woman? It is a fine and beautiful thing that she has done for me.' (Verse 10)

Eyore was feeling more gloomy than usual. It was his birthday, and nobody had noticed. Then along came Winnie-the-Pooh, who was really a very kind bear. 'Stay there,' he said to Eeyore, and hurried home to find a present. He chose quite a small jar of honey from his cupboard and set off back to Eeyore. Suddenly a terrible hunger came over him. Forgetting Eeyore, forgetting everything but his own tummy, he ate every bit of honey. All that was left for Eeyore was an empty jar.

The jar that the woman brought to Jesus was full of very expensive perfume. It was the loveliest thing she had. She didn't think about herself at all, only about Jesus. Somehow she knew what would happen to him, and she wanted to show her love.

A slippery slope
Matthew 26:14-25

Judas, the traitor, spoke up. 'Surely, Teacher, you don't mean me?' he asked. Jesus answered, 'So you say.' (Verse 25)

Have you ever tried running fast down a steep hill that's covered in bits of stone? (It's called a 'scree'.) At first it's fun. The wind whistles past your ears and you feel you're flying like a bird. Wheee! Then you try to stop and you can't. You've lost control of yourself and finish up in a heap at the bottom.

This is what was happening to Judas. He'd decided that Jesus wasn't going the way he wanted, so he started on his slippery slope. He went to the chief priests and 'sold' Jesus. Then he went back to Jesus and tried to behave normally.

Judas was slipping; he'd lost control of himself. He even looked at Jesus and said, 'Surely you don't mean me?' No stopping now. Nothing but trouble ahead for Judas.

A meal to remember
Matthew 26:26-30

While they were eating, Jesus took a piece of bread, gave a prayer of thanks, broke it, and gave it to his disciples. 'Take and eat it,' he said; 'this is my body.' (Verse 26)

The meal that Jesus shared in Jerusalem with his friends was a very special meal.

I remember a special meal on a faraway Scottish island. We were leading a working party of teenagers. During the day we dug ditches, milked goats, sheared sheep. In the evening we read the Bible, talked about it, prayed and sang.

One evening, all twenty of us gathered round the kitchen table. We said prayers, then slowly we passed round an ordinary loaf of bread. Each person broke off a small piece and ate it. Then we passed round a cup of wine and each of us had a sip.

We were remembering that meal in Jerusalem, and Jesus was with us on that Scottish island just as surely as he had been with his friends in Jerusalem.

Matthew 25:14—26:30

Things to do

Bread and God

In monasteries, monks are sometimes silent at mealtimes, so when they want bread they make the sign shown in picture 'A'. Did you know that this is the same as their sign for God, only the other way up? (Picture 'B'.)

If you can think of a sign for cornflakes, orange juice and chocolate spread, you could have a silent breakfast!

Toby + Trish — Missed it!

Breakfast finished an hour ago. We ate quietly so as not to wake you up!

I really mean it
Matthew 26:31-35

Peter answered, 'I will never say that, even if I have to die with you!' And all the other disciples said the same thing. (Verse 35)

How many times have we said we'll do a thing and then, somehow, we don't. Maybe we've promised to clean out the hamster's cage, or tidy our bedroom, but it just doesn't get done. Perhaps a friend calls, or we go out, or we just forget. Whatever the reason, the result's the same. But we really meant it at the time.

When Peter said he would never leave Jesus, or deny knowing him, he really meant it at the time. He truly loved Jesus. He of all people would never let Jesus down. He would be proud to be a friend of Jesus, no matter what followed.

Lord Jesus, make me brave to do what I want to do for you... no matter what follows.

Agony
Matthew 26:36-46

Jesus said to them, 'The sorrow in my heart is so great that it almost crushes me. Stay here and keep watch with me.' (Verse 38)

Gethsemane was a lovely cool shelter of trees during the heat of the day, and at night its stillness wrapped round you like a blanket.

Olive trees grew there, with soft, silvery-green leaves. Olive trees live for hundreds, even thousands, of years, and as they age, their black trunks become gnarled and twisted with the effort of getting water from the dry soil. They look as though they're writhing in agony. Yet an olive branch is a symbol of peace, because they take so long to grow, and last for such a long time.

Jesus was in an agony of sadness. He knew what would happen to him; that is why he came. There was no way out.

Yet, like the olive tree, from his agony would come a peace that would last.

Dark deeds
Matthew 26:47-56

Judas went straight to Jesus and said, 'Peace be with you, Teacher,' and kissed him. (Verse 49)

Judas had finally reached the end of his plunge down the slippery slope. He had hit the bottom. He'd taken two beautiful things and destroyed them: teacher—someone to admire and respect; and a kiss—a sign of love. With these he betrayed Jesus.

Imagine... the quiet garden... Jesus waiting and praying. Then suddenly they come. Loud voices. Flaring torches. The tramp of feet. It must have seemed like a nightmare to the disciples. All these people, armed, to capture one man.

But the man they came for was not an ordinary man. Even the priests and elders knew that. There could be no mistakes. Jesus had to be dealt with quickly—now.

And God, in his love for you and me, allowed it to begin.

94

The trials
Matthew 26:57-68

The chief priests and the whole Council tried to find some false evidence against Jesus to put him to death; but they could not find any, even though many people came forward and told lies about him. (Verses 59 and 60)

In our country, a trial is a serious matter. Strict rules have to be kept and the judge will not take sides while the evidence is being heard. Witnesses swear on the Bible to tell the truth and the prisoner is considered innocent until he or she is proved guilty.

The trial of Jesus was not like that. It was no trial at all. The high priest, the teachers of the law and the elders broke every rule—they were desperate. Jesus was tried during the night, which was against the rules. Witnesses had been given money to tell lies. Worst of all, Jesus was considered guilty right from the start.

Yet, amid the hatred and the lies, the hurt and the mockery, Jesus stood calmly waiting for the verdict.

Peter doesn't know Jesus
Matthew 26:69-75

Then Peter said, 'I swear that I am telling the truth! May God punish me if I am not! I do not know that man!' (Verse 74)

'I saw you do it.' 'No, you didn't.' 'Yes, I did.' 'I didn't do it.' Two people arguing. You've probably heard something like it yourself. One of them is telling a lie, and whichever one it is knows he or she is lying. They'll have their reasons, but a lie isn't easy to live with.

Peter knew he was lying. His reason was that he was terribly frightened—for himself. What if the same thing happened to him that was happening to Jesus? So he lied, to save himself.

God didn't punish Peter, but he allowed Peter to punish himself. When the cock crowed three times, Peter realized what he'd done. Even worse... Jesus had known that he would do it. And this big strong man broke down and cried.

117

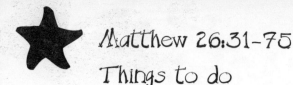

Matthew 26:31-75

Things to do

Jesus all alone

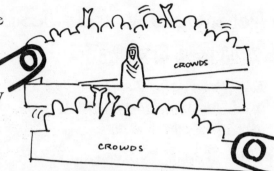

CROWDS

CROWDS

Although Jesus was surrounded by shouting, angry crowds, he was very much alone in those dreadful hours after he was arrested. Use the following activity to help you to imagine the scene.

Cut a piece of thin A4 card into three equal widthways sections. Draw the angry crowds on two pieces. Turn the third piece lengthways and draw a picture of Jesus as shown in the picture. Fold back the tabs and stand the figure on a table. Hold the 'crowd' cards behind and in front of the figure and move them up and down.

Toby + Trish — Not alone

All of a sudden I'm in bed and the door is shut. Now it's just me and Jesus for the night!

If only...
Matthew 27:1-5

'I have sinned by betraying an innocent man to death!' Judas said. 'What do we care about that?' they answered. 'That is your business!' (Verse 4)

Have you ever thought, 'If only...'? 'If only I hadn't been so rude to Mum yesterday.' 'If only I'd prepared better for that test we had at school.' 'If only I hadn't eaten so much at the party.' Results— sad Mum, failed test, tummy-ache. Try to think of other times when you wish you'd done things differently. But we can't put the clock back and have another go. What's done is done, and we must face up to the results.

Judas thought, 'If only...' but it was too late. He tried to put things right, but it was too late. Jesus had been condemned to death, and he'd helped to make it happen. How could he face up to the results of what he'd done? There was no putting the clock back for Judas. 'If only...'

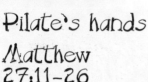

Pilate's hands
Matthew 27:11-26

When Pilate saw that it was no use to go on, but that a riot might break out, he took some water, washed his hands in front of the crowd, and said, 'I am not responsible for the death of this man! This is your doing!' (Verse 24)

Four hundred years ago, William Shakespeare wrote plays that were so popular they're still performed all over the world. One of them, 'Macbeth', is about a man who wanted to be king of Scotland. He and his wife killed the rightful king and Macbeth became king. But the Macbeths weren't happy. 'All the water in the sea couldn't wash my hands clean,' moaned Macbeth. And Lady Macbeth took to sleep-walking, pretending to wash her hands as she went.

Pilate had a problem. He could see that Jesus was innocent, but if he set him free there'd be a riot. So he sentenced Jesus to death. Then he washed his hands in front of the people, showing that it wasn't his fault. But washing your hands doesn't make you clean inside. Pilate would never forget that awful day.

Jesus is crucified
Matthew 27:27-44

Above his head they put the written notice of the accusation against him: 'This is Jesus, the King of the Jews.' (Verse 37)

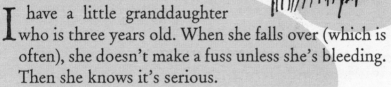

I have a little granddaughter who is three years old. When she falls over (which is often), she doesn't make a fuss unless she's bleeding. Then she knows it's serious.

Jesus was bleeding... a lot. And hurting. He'd been mocked and beaten, spat on and insulted. Then they knelt and mocked again: 'Long live the King of the Jews.' They nailed him to a cross and fastened a notice on it: 'This is Jesus, the King of the Jews.'

Then they crowded round to watch, elbowing for a better view, shouting. Others walked past, not caring. There in front were the chief priests and elders. They'd got what they wanted. 'Isn't he the king of Israel?' they jeered. What a way to treat a king!

And God, who was hurting too, let it happen. Why?

Jesus dies
Matthew 27:45-56

At about three o'clock Jesus cried out with a loud shout... 'My God, my God, why did you abandon me?' (Verse 46)

There was so much happening on that hill outside Jerusalem. Three men hanging on crosses, a crowd watching and jeering, soldiers on guard in case of trouble.

But nobody saw the most important thing of all. That was a matter just between Jesus and his heavenly Father. 'My God, why did you abandon me?' cried Jesus. For the first time ever, Jesus was cut off from his Father.

At that moment, Jesus took the blame for all the wickedness—cruelty, lying, hatred, dishonesty, envy—that ever has been and ever will be. And it separated him from God. Jesus' arms, spread wide on the cross, show just how much he loves us... so much. He opened up the way so that we, you and I, need never know separation from God.

The end?
Matthew 27:57–66

So Joseph took Jesus' body, wrapped it in a new linen sheet, and placed it in his own tomb, which he had just recently dug out of solid rock. Then he rolled a large stone across the entrance to the tomb and went away. (Verses 59–60)

It says a lot about how Pilate was feeling that he handed over the body of Jesus to Joseph. Normally, people who had been crucified were not allowed a proper burial. It was Pilate's way of saying 'sorry'— a bit too late.

It also says a lot about how the priests and Pharisees were feeling when they wanted a guard put on the tomb. Already a huge stone blocked the entrance—so huge that Joseph would have needed help to put it in place. But even though the priests and Pharisees had seen Jesus hanging on the cross, had seen him die, these awful men were still frightened of what he might do. It looked like the end of Jesus, but they couldn't forget him and what he had said.

Matthew 27:1-66

Things to do

Cross over

Just as you can cross over a bridge, Jesus made it possible by his death and resurrection for us to *cross over* from the darkness of being separated from God into the sunshine of being with God all the time.

On a large piece of paper, paint a picture of a deep river with darkness on the left and sunshine on the right. Draw a picture of the cross in the middle. Paint in a bridge crossing the river from the darkness into the sunshine, or collect some wooden ice-lolly sticks and glue them on to your picture to make a bridge.

Toby + Trish — Safely across

Our lollipop man is a bit like Jesus, seeing us safely across

The beginning
Matthew 28:1-7

The angel spoke to the women. 'You must not be afraid,' he said. 'I know you are looking for Jesus, who was crucified. He is not here; he has been raised, just as he said. Come here and see the place where he was lying.' (Verses 5–6)

One of my favourite books is *The Lion, the Witch and the Wardrobe* by C.S. Lewis. The country of Narnia had been in the power of the White Witch for a long time. It was always winter, with snow and ice—everything seemed dead. Then, because of the coming of Aslan, a very special lion, the snow and ice began to melt. Streams started to chatter and splash. Everything came to life again in a lovely, fresh way.

It must have felt like that on the first Easter morning in the garden where the tomb was. After all the awfulness and cruelty, the darkness, the pain and sadness, Jesus had come to life again. The tomb was empty. Everything was lovely and fresh... a new beginning.

First, 'Come and see,' said the angel. Then, 'Go quickly and tell the others.'

It's not the end after all!

Jesus lives!
Matthew 28:8-14

So the women left the tomb in a hurry, afraid and yet filled with joy, and ran to tell his disciples. (Verse 8)

When things are happening around you that you can't understand, you feel afraid. The two Marys found it hard to believe what they had just seen and heard. They felt afraid.

But at the same time, there was this wonderful feeling of happiness and their hearts soared up like a bird. They had seen the angel and the empty tomb. The angel's words were still echoing in their ears. Fear and happiness were tangled together as they hurried to tell the disciples.

Then they met Jesus, and he understood how they felt. 'Don't be afraid,' he said, and only happiness was left. Jesus was alive—the same Jesus whom they knew and loved. Yet there was something different. They fell on their knees and worshipped him as their Lord and their God.

Jesus is alive again!

With us for always
Matthew 28:16–20

'And I will be with you always, to the end of the age.' (Verse 20b)

What a marvellous ending to Matthew's Gospel—on a hill in Galilee, maybe a hill they'd often climbed with Jesus. Imagine the disciples waiting in the sunshine, looking down at the places where they'd been with Jesus, looking back at what had happened there.

Imagine their joy when Jesus came to them—their friend, and now the Lord of heaven and earth. But the time for looking back was over. Now they must look forward and tell everyone the good news of Jesus' love.

Matthew's Gospel starts with a promise: 'You will name him Jesus, because he will save his people from their sins.' Jesus has done that. And now Matthew ends with a wonderful promise from Jesus: 'I will be with you always, to the end of the age.' What more can we ask?